SERVICE LEARNING FOR TEENS™

ENDING HUNGER AND HOMELESSNESS
THROUGH SERVICE LEARNING

KATHY FURGANG

ROSEN
PUBLISHING®

New York

Published in 2015 by The Rosen Publishing Group, Inc.
29 East 21st Street, New York, NY 10010

First Edition

Library of Congress Cataloging-in-Publication Data

Furgang, Kathy.
Ending hunger and homelessness through service learning/Kathy Furgang.
    pages cm.—(Service learning for teens)
Includes bibliographical references and index.
ISBN 978-1-4777-7959-0 (library bound)
1. Service learning—Juvenile literature. 2. Social action—Juvenile literature. 3. Food relief—Juvenile literature. 4. Homelessness—Juvenile literature. I. Title.
LC220.5.F86 2014
361.3'7—dc23

                                                    2014010946

Manufactured in the United States of America

CONTENTS

INTRODUCTION

Homeless Alone
Hungry & Cold!
All Acts of Kindness
greatly Appreciated
Thank you. Cheers

Hunger and homelessness are among the most serious challenges of poverty throughout North America.

As Benjamin Franklin, one of the Founding Fathers of the United States, once said, "Doing nothing for others is the undoing of ourselves." Anyone who has seen hungry or homeless people on city streets, or anywhere throughout North America, is likely to be touched by the hardship her or she sees. Helping those in need is one of the noblest pursuits, and it can be rewarding, as well. "How wonderful it is that nobody need wait a single moment before starting to improve the world," wrote thirteen-year-old Anne Frank in her diary while living in hiding in Nazi-occupied Holland.

But what can someone do to help improve the conditions of people living with hunger and homelessness? Curing the conditions of poverty that exist in our society is a job that even the most experienced politicians and economists struggle with. What can just one person do to help those in need?

You may say that donating food to a food pantry or volunteering for a few hours in a homeless shelter is something that could help the situation. After all, students don't have much time to spare, since they are required to spend most of their day in school. The time left for public service and helping the community is cut down considerably after students' academic responsibilities are met. However, with the educational tool called service learning, students can combine classroom instruction with meaningful community service.

A growing number of schools are incorporating service learning into their curriculum. As a result, a class can do projects in math, social studies, science, and English—or even home economics, music, and foreign language studies—that incorporate learning and projects about community service. This type of curriculum heightens the students' sense of community and gets them engaged with a sense of service and civic responsibility. The personal sense of responsibility and satisfaction that students receive from service learning is also extremely rewarding.

Through service learning, students can serve their communities and become civically minded while also exploring their required school curriculum. Some specialties of service learning concentrate on protecting the environment or improving community health and safety. Other areas of concentration may include supporting the elderly, the disabled, or veterans and military families.

In the following sections, you will learn about ways that service learning can help people suffering from hunger and homelessness. These examples can provide good starting points for your own exploration into service learning. If your school already incorporates service learning into its curriculum, you may be inspired with some new ideas regarding the prevention of hunger and homelessness. If your school does not incorporate service-learning components, there are ways you can work with community groups, such as scouting groups, to plan and carry out service-learning projects. Either way, incorporating academics with community service can be a win-win situation for both students and the community.

CHAPTER ONE

READY TO SERVE

Most people think of going to school as sitting behind a desk and listening to a teacher talk, reading textbooks, doing assignments, and taking tests on each subject covered. While this is still an accurate way to describe many schools, an increasing number of schools are introducing new and interesting ways to challenge students and help them become active in their communities.

RECENT HISTORY OF SERVICE LEARNING

How did service learning make its way into schools and communities across the nation? Americans have served their communities and helped others in the United States since colonial days. But the introduction of service learning began with legislation that President George H. W. Bush signed in 1990. The National and Community Service Act of 1990 created a new and independent federal agency called the Commission on National and Community Service. One of the areas this commission was dedicated to promote was service learning for school-aged children.

When politicians pass legislation such as this, it can have a far-reaching effect on the community as well as on the lives of the children who participate. Most students have no idea what they want to accomplish when they grow up, but introducing them to experiences that they would normally not have in

President Bill Clinton signed the National and Community Service Trust Act of 1993. The legislation promoted community service for students.

school opens their horizons wider than ever and helps them to consider ideas they may not have thought of for years—if ever. Jayci Angell, who worked on a service-learning project at Parkview High School with the help of a program through Missouri State University, said of the experience, "I would recommend service learning to others because it is a great chance to get involved with the community and really put into action what you are learning. It gives necessary experience for deciding on career paths and is very valuable."

Additional legislation included the National and Community Service Trust Act of 1993, signed into law by President Bill Clinton. This legislation created the Corporation for National and Community Service. As a result, Learn and Serve America was launched, which is a government service that provides grants upon request to help schools and community organizations to set up service-learning programs.

INTEGRATION OF ACADEMICS AND COMMUNITY NEEDS

The National and Community Service Trust Act of 1993 also defined what service learning is and how it should be properly and actively participated in. In addition to meeting the needs of the community, a service-learning project must also integrate the academic curriculum of students. This means that the project must incorporate as many school subjects as possible. For example, if your service-learning project includes working at a soup kitchen, math can be incorporated. How many pounds of potatoes, turkey, or stuffing would be needed to serve five hundred people? How many gallons of milk or juice would be needed for the same group? If monetary donations were given to the soup kitchen, how much food would the donations buy? How much would the food weigh, and how would this influence the way you planned to transport the food?

The curriculum integration shouldn't stop at math. In social studies, your class may study past legislation related to homelessness. You can research local, state, and national laws about homelessness or homeless shelters. The history of homeless shelters would be useful to know, and you may wish to find out how other countries handle their homelessness problems to make a comparison.

 ## RECOGNIZING A NEED

In addition to the classroom learning about hunger or homelessness, students should try to recognize a need in their community. Students in Wicomico County, Maryland, learned about manufacturing technology in their textile class. Instead of making something for themselves in the class, students applied what they learned to help meet the needs of the community. The textile students used their new skills to make and donate one hundred fleece hats to a local crisis center.

An art class may choose to make a mural that can hang in a food pantry or homeless shelter to brighten the décor. Students can make pottery to be used at the shelters. Home economics classes may choose projects that can be donated to the hungry or homeless rather than kept for themselves.

In science classes, learning about nutrition can help students reflect on the needs of the community.

Service-learning students incorporate educational learning experiences in science, health, and many other subjects while also serving the community.

Learning about your local soil and the best fruits and vegetables to grow in your area can help a service-learning group plan a project around a sustainable garden to feed the hungry.

THE SERVICE-LEARNING PROCESS

There are five core steps in the service-learning process: investigation, planning, action, reflection, and demonstration. Exploring these five steps can help those who are interested in service learning to brainstorm ideas and get a sense of how the process of service learning works.

 TAKE SMALL STEPS

Many of the steps required for service learning can be overwhelming, but taking these steps one at a time can help to address smaller issues and get students thinking. At a high school in Humble, Texas, students did a math project in which they developed a monthly budget based on a family who lived on a minimum-wage salary. This helped them realize the everyday effects of poverty, and the project fit into their larger community service-learning project. While this was not a full-reaching community project that incorporated all academic subjects, the math exercise helped them to focus on a problem and apply real-life solutions.

INVESTIGATION

Before any service project is planned or begins, some thoughtful collaboration about the needs of the community must be undertaken. The investigation stage of service learning is like dipping your toes in the water to learn what your community needs, why it is needed, and what could be done to help the situation. You can investigate by reading the news about problems in your community. You may see a news report on television about a rise in homelessness in your area or an increase in unemployment or hunger in your community. The investigation stage is like a social analysis of the situation that allows you to decide whether it is a topic or idea that you would like to pursue.

Investigating may mean taking action beyond observing your world. While investigation may start out as a personal, direct observation of hunger or homelessness in your community or the world, you may need to dig deeper. Interviews with experts can help to make the investigation stage valuable. You may wish to interview people who work at a food pantry or homeless shelter to learn more about the needs of the clients they serve. How often are people served? How much food is used in a single day? Where do people go after they have eaten their meals? How long are people allowed to stay at a shelter? The answers to these questions can help prompt ideas to guide the planning of your project.

For instance, during your investigation, you may find that food pantries are overflowing with donations around the holidays, but they struggle to get enough food at other times of the year. This may affect the decisions you make about how you would like to approach your service-learning project. Would you provide help to collect, store, or serve extra food during the hectic holiday season, or would you concentrate on generating more food items to sustain them during downtimes? In addition, you may find from your investigation stage that local food pantries or homeless shelters may not allow the services you hope to offer. Instead of planning a service-learning idea that is not possible, use the investigation stage to see if there are community members who will work with you through the process. Investigate what is possible, what is allowed, and what will be the most enjoyable for your group.

The investigation stage is also a great time to think outside of the box and decide how each curriculum area can be fully utilized in a unique way. Brainstorm ways that you can learn about hunger and homelessness through your curriculum areas. Think of ways to integrate as many topics as you can, and think about what will be needed to pursue each idea.

PLANNING

Once you have investigated possible service-learning projects, it's time to choose one and investigate it further. Beginning the planning stages may mean conducting further research. According to the National Association of Secondary School Principals, there are many ways to do this. Eighth graders at New York State's Mineola High School worked together with an

Teamwork, planning, and problem solving are important parts of the service-learning process.

eleventh-grade class and made a timeline of the history of hunger in the United States, including government and community responses during each stage. This additional research into their topic helped them to assess what had been done in the past and create their own plans and solutions to the problem.

Students who are considering a project related to hunger may continue their research by reading books or articles about low-income areas that are considered "food deserts." These are urban or rural areas that lack good access to nutritious foods. A food desert does not mean that an area has no access to food, but the access may be only convenience stores with no fresh produce or ingredients that a family or individual would need to cook nutritious meals. Researching how some areas have solved this problem can help students in their own service-learning planning.

Another part of the planning stage is to strategize about what would be needed to carry out a service-learning project. An art class can plan advertising posters for the project, and students can decide where to hang the posters.

Clarifying the steps that students will take and the roles that students and teachers will play in the project is essential to a successful plan. For some schools, especially when younger students are involved, it may seem that the planning stage should be handled largely by a teacher. However, the more involved students can be in their own project, the more interested they are likely to be in the process and the results. Ask your teacher how you can get involved in the planning stage and coordination of the project.

ACTION

The next stage of the process is to put the service-learning plans into purposeful action. This usually means going out into the community to put your plan into motion. You have likely worked with community members to make sure your plan will be permitted, but remember that the community you interact with should be aware that you are working on a service-learning project. This demonstrates a mutual agreement between the people involved and a respect for the partnership that you have.

These fourth and fifth graders are handing out pre-wrapped gifts at the holidays to help local families in their town of Flint, Michigan.

Commitment to the plan is also very important. If you planned to commit a certain number of hours per week working at a food pantry or homeless shelter, you should do your best to meet your commitment. If you planned to commit to a gardening project from seed to harvest, you must follow through. It is understandable that you may not be able to make every outing due to personal commitments, but it is smart to have a plan in place for when students cannot meet their obligations. Sometimes, service-learning projects are done during school hours, which may make the problem of commitment less of an issue. But when students are expected to meet on evenings or weekends, it is a good idea to have flexible schedules and back-up plans.

The "action" stage of the service-learning project is often the most memorable and rewarding for many students. Ashley Brendel, who worked with the Missouri State University program on a project through the Multiple Sclerosis Society, states, "[Service learning] allows you to get professional experience that you can't get in a classroom setting. The firsthand experience is awesome!" The very idea of service learning is to help students get out of the classroom and into their communities to do what they can to help others.

REFLECTION

We often think of a reflection as something we do at the end of a project, but in the case of service learning, reflection can also help connect each stage of the process and make it more rewarding for students.

Reflecting on the project along the way helps students be more self-aware. It helps students keep their plans on track and make changes when necessary. Reflection also helps students understand what they are learning and how the project is impacting the community.

Reflection at the end of a project is just as important. Students can ask themselves the following questions when reflecting on a project: How did I help the community? What did I learn about hunger or homelessness? Is there more I can do to address the problem? Was our project the best it could be? What did others learn from the experience?

Many students write reflective essays about their experiences with the project, and these can be used to teach other students about service learning and its impact on communities. The reflection stage is important because it allows students to take the time they need to consider the issue they chose to explore in the first place.

DEMONSTRATION

The demonstration stage is an important way to spread knowledge about hunger, homelessness, and finding a solution to a community's problems. Students can share photos of their experiences in a slideshow, or they can share their reflection essays with other students. Each curriculum subject that students worked in can incorporate ways that students can show what they learned.

The demonstrations that students provide for their peers can spark an idea in other students that may help lead to the next project idea. Teachers can save demonstrations and show them to new classes who are beginning the process. Inspiration can come from student demonstrations. When students see what others have accomplished, they can use that as a springboard for their own learning and investigations into trying to end hunger and homelessness.

CHAPTER TWO

STAMPING OUT HUNGER

The statistics about hunger are frightening. In the United States, one in six people faces hunger.

A person who faces hunger or consistent inadequate food due to lack of money or other resources is considered by the U.S. Department of Agriculture (USDA) to be "food insecure." As a result of the Great Recession that began in 2007, the number of food-insecure American households has increased greatly. Food insecurity affects 17.9 million households. This problem is not due to a lack of available food. In fact, about 40 percent of food in the United States is thrown out each year. All that wasted food is worth about $165 billion and could feed twenty-five million people.

Poverty is the reason for the increase in food-insecure households. The risk of hunger increases with minority groups who traditionally belong to lower economic groups. Nationwide, one in five American children are at risk of hunger. Among African-American and Latino children, however, the number is one in three.

There are seven states that have food insecurity rates over 15 percent. They are Mississippi, Texas, Arkansas, Alabama, Georgia, Florida, and North Carolina. What is

Actor Dean Cain hands out food with the National Coalition for the Homeless in New York City, raising awareness of the city's hunger problem.

done to help people who face hunger? Approximately one in seven people receive assistance from the Supplemental Nutrition Assistance Program (SNAP). About half of these people are children. But does this solve the problem? When the economy performs poorly, cuts to these government services are often reduced, and some programs may be eliminated. This can lead to problems worsening over time.

> ## BUMPY ROAD

Recent changes to a piece of legislation, the Farm Bill, called for further cuts to the benefits that food-insecure families in America receive through food stamps, or SNAP (Supplemental Nutrition Assistance Program). What does this mean for people who are already struggling for food resources? It can mean an increase in families and individuals at food banks or soup kitchens. It can mean a shortage of food available at these facilities. It can mean a need for increased funding to community programs. This all translates into a greater need for community service volunteers in the future. When government funding cannot meet the needs of the people, often citizens must volunteer to fill in the gaps.

Hunger is also an issue in Canada. Every month, close to 850,000 Canadians are assisted by food banks, and more than 36 percent of these people are children. About half of the people who received food-bank assistance also receive social assistance from the Canadian government. Relying on the government for assistance can have its drawbacks in Canada, as well. In recent years, 8 percent of food banks ran out of food, and 50 percent had to cut back on the amount of food provided to each household.

What can students do to analyze and address the problem of hunger? Studying its history and effects can be a great start. Next, analyzing the needs in your own community can lead you to varied and inspiring ideas about how to help people from food-insecure households.

FOLLOW THE LEADER

Before digging into your own plan, consider what others have done so that you can be inspired by their ideas and also allow them to help you brainstorm your own ideas. The Maryland Department of Education is one of the nation's leading examples of how to bring service-learning education to students. The state has shared many good examples of service learning on various websites so that others can benefit from what Maryland students have done.

For example, some schools have joined with a nonprofit, grassroots organization called Empty Bowls. Maryland public schools have created an annual Empty Bowls project as part of their service-learning curriculum. In a middle school in Charles County, for example, students learn about hunger in their world and community as part of their social studies classes. They also work in art classes to design, make, and paint ceramic bowls. The bowls are used at a charity dinner that takes place in the community. The community donates money, and local restaurants donate food. The money raised by the dinner is donated to the local Red Cross chapter. The event combines curriculum learning from various subject matters, and the students take action to help the community.

Projects can be flexible and emphasize the subjects where you have the most help, resources, and

An artist demonstrates the process of making pottery for people attending an Empty Bowls event in Columbia, Maryland.

guidance. A high school in Frederick County, Maryland, also takes part in an Empty Bowls project. The students plan their service learning differently than the students in Charles County. The Frederick County students incorporate their character education curriculum in their projects. They use their planning and coordination skills to take a larger part in planning the events. Students from different grade levels work together. Some grades contribute the empty bowls, while others handle fundraising or planning. The coordination between groups can be rewarding and also allows students to take part in a large-scale project. Remember that larger projects involving many grade levels will require more adult supervision and guidance in order to be coordinated correctly. The planning of the size and scope of your project can be part of the investigation and planning stages.

Using the ideas of other schools as a springboard can help students figure out what they need to make their project work. Look at several models before you begin your own. Think about whether you will be working with as many people as the model you studied. How will your project be similar or different? This type

 JOURNAL REFLECTIONS

As you have read, reflection is one of the five stages of service learning. You can incorporate reflection many times throughout your project to keep track of your progress. You may wish to keep a journal as part of your own personal reflections on the experience. Many students have fond memories of their service-learning experiences, and the experience provides a foundation for involvement in community service they may have later in life. A journal can provide students with a long-lasting memory of the experience and be a great documentation of community change.

of thought process can help you determine how many people you will need for your project and how the different tasks can be assigned and tracked.

Remember to be creative. Many Empty Bowls projects may use the bowls as a symbol of hunger, but they can be practical as well. Bowls made using the right type of finish can be used for eating. Donating bowls to a food pantry or soup kitchen is a good way to show your support and be remembered in the community. Thinking of small ways to improve projects can be rewarding. Use the reflection time between stages to help you make small adjustments and improvements.

BLAZE YOUR OWN PATH

Using other projects as a guide can be a good way for students to gain experience with service learning. Other students may have more experience with community service and wish to create their own project. For example, your investigation stage may reveal that you live near an area considered to be a food desert. Your research reveals that this means an increased chance of food-insecure households in the area. After brainstorming with your group, you may decide that a community garden is a good way to bring nutritious foods to the neighborhood at little or no cost to the neighbors. You may even find research that shows that the more resources that residents of a low-income neighborhood can be given to help sustain their own food supplies, the more food secure the households in the neighborhood will be.

Instead of just feeding the homeless, schools may plant gardens to help the homeless on a long-term basis.

A community garden can be a rewarding project, but it can also be ambitious depending on the number of students you are working with and the adult guidance you have available. Your investigation and planning stages may involve contacting a local gardener to find out what is needed in terms of physical labor, time commitment, and seasonal timing for the project.

Interviews with community leaders can help determine where a garden may be placed, what kind of work would be needed to clear the area for garden use, and how the community would gain access to and possibly help maintain the site.

Back at school, your science teacher would be a great resource for finding out about the local soil and the types of seeds that grow at different times of the year. Put your math hat on to figure out the cost of the seeds you want to grow and the amount of space you will need to grow each type of seed. Remember that you must also calculate the distances required between each seed planting into the amount of space you will need. Consider as many details as you can when planning your garden, such as access to water, sunlight, or shade, depending on the plants you are growing.

Once you have finished your basic planning, you may have to work with an English teacher to prepare a detailed proposal that is presented to the town for permission. This may require attending town-planning meetings to present your proposal to board members. Being prepared with historical and economic statistics about hunger can help you make your point. Examples of successful community gardens should be presented as well. If your plan is approved, it may be time to take action.

COOK UP A PLAN

Suppose your service-learning project for a community garden is a big hit. The community has more than enough food to keep itself sustainable, and the residents may even help to maintain the garden and grow more food in the future. How can you top that? Another way to stamp out hunger and help the food-insecure households in your community is to make sure that people know how to use their food to make nutritious meals.

Relying on food pantries is likely a last resort for many families, so teaching people to use the products of

Service learning for the hungry and homeless may involve classes in nutrition and cooking—including learning how the tear ducts react when slicing an onion!

a sustainable garden is a great way to offer something valuable to your community. Cooking used to be a skill that was passed from generation to generation, but with the popularity of processed foods, this art has been lost in many families. Processed foods can be less expensive than fresh foods, but they are often far less nutritious. This is why cooking must return as a survival skill for people who want to provide nutritious food.

A service-learning plan that promotes cooking is a natural match to coordinate with a home economics teacher. A few simple recipes can be developed, and students can practice them at school. Next, holding a few cooking classes at a food pantry or other public facility with a kitchen can be a great way to connect with the community.

Art classes can help students create advertising posters. Math classes can help them calculate the amount of food they will need to make a certain number of servings of a meal. Reflecting on your project and demonstrating its success can be a rewarding experience that can influence others.

CHAPTER THREE
HALTING HOMELESSNESS

The effects of homelessness are far reaching. Homelessness in families can cause children distress. Homelessness in our towns shows that our communities have social and economic issues that must be dealt with.

According to the National Law Center on Homelessness and Poverty, there are more than 1.75 million homeless people in the United States. If we look deeper into this number, we can learn some fascinating details. Poverty is a major factor in the problem of homelessness. About 25 percent of homeless people actually have jobs. But there are also other issues lurking beneath the surface. About 66 percent of the homeless population in the United States has problems with alcohol, drug abuse, or mental illness. About 40 percent of homeless people are military veterans. And about 46 percent of American cities report that domestic violence is a major cause of homelessness among its citizens. The combination of all of these factors makes homelessness a serious issue that deserves careful study.

Homelessness affects families as well as individuals. Poverty, substance abuse, and mental illness are leading causes of homelessness in North America.

LOOKING INTO YOUR COMMUNITY

For students interested in service learning to help the homeless, the investigation stage can be enlightening. Find out how homelessness affects your community. Find out if shelters exist in your hometown or surrounding area. Sometimes shelters exist without the public knowing much about their history or the services they provide. Find out when the shelter opened and under what circumstances. When you look into the history of homelessness in the United States, you will find that shelters have existed since the late 1800s. Jane Addams was one of the pioneers of housing those in need. In 1889, she and Ellen Gates Starr co-founded a settlement house for recently arrived European immigrants on the West Side of Chicago. These immigrants faced

Volunteers help at missions and homeless shelters. This volunteer helps children celebrate the holidays with face painting.

poverty, hunger, and homelessness in large numbers, and Addams and Starr's Hull House became a landmark of hope for the American dream.

Helping the homeless population has often been a complicated and difficult political and economic issue. Budget cuts often make their way to social services before other areas of government aid. Even the historic Hull House suffered from increased operating costs, and in 2012, it was forced to close its doors for good.

Students can learn a lot by exploring how homeless shelters and other public facilities receive their funding. There are differences on the local, state, and federal levels, so learning the histories and economics behind each category can help focus your service-learning plans.

DOING YOUR BEST

Some students may find working with the homeless to be an emotional or even a disturbing experience. They may feel that their efforts are not making the difference they thought they would. Remember that you're not trying to solve world problems in your middle school or high school classes. You are simply trying to learn more about important societal issues while giving back to the community.

Providing assistance in a community service capacity can open your eyes to problems that you did not know existed in your community. Your contributions are worth the effort, even if not a single person finds a home because of your work. Sarah Cecchettini of Parkview High School worked on a service-learning project through Missouri State University and realized

DIRECT VS. INDIRECT SERVICE

In service learning, there are two ways to help the community. One is through direct service, which means that you work one-on-one with the community that you are helping. Direct service can mean serving meals at a soup kitchen or helping community members set up a garden. The other way you can help a community is through indirect service. With indirect service, you do not work one-on-one with the community. You may help by collecting food for a food drive or putting together toiletry bags for a homeless shelter. Your efforts may raise money, resources, or awareness, but you do not have direct contact with the hungry or homeless populations you are helping. Both methods of community service are acceptable in meeting the requirements of a service-learning project.

the importance of the project. "I think that all students should give back to the community while in school," she said. "Everyone needs to focus on others at some point and help their community."

LOOK FOR STANDOUT MODELS

When looking for service-learning projects related to homeless populations, consider what other students have done. The Maryland Department of Education has a project called Flavors and Favors for students ranging from elementary through high school age. The mission of this project is to teach students about advocacy for the homeless population and homelessness prevention. As part of their work, students provide decorative food bags and food baskets filled with paper goods and food for local families in need. The project is easily adaptable for different ages. The exercise combines their social studies curriculum for citizenship with their art and organizational skills. The project also gives students something to reflect on when they think about what is at stake for the families who can no longer pay their rent or mortgage.

A similar project was created in Calvert County, Maryland, for elementary school students to get involved by providing the basic needs to homeless people. Each grade level was responsible for collecting basic essentials, such as toothbrushes, shampoo, or combs. The items were then donated to a local homeless shelter.

Some projects go beyond the local level and make students aware that homelessness is a global problem. In Maryland's Anne Arundel County, middle school students created a project called Poverty to Prosperity. Students collected and recycled used athletic shoes by selling them in Ghana, Africa. The profits from the project were used to establish a scholarship fund for rural farming families in West Africa.

Students in Montgomery County, Maryland, looked to the nation's capital to address the problem of

Students often work with other adults, teachers, or advisers when they volunteer at food banks or homeless shelters.

homelessness. Their investigation stage revealed that having prepared foods ready to hand out at soup kitchens was a challenge for the workers and presented a problem for the people trying to use the facility. The students planned and coordinated an event during which 100 students made more than 750 sandwiches for D.C. Central Kitchen in the District of Columbia.

In Howard County, a middle school and high school project was developed that focused mainly on the math curriculum. Students learned about the business concepts of profit and loss, gross and net, and discounts and taxes. After conducting a fundraiser, they used the profits to purchase food that they turned into bag lunches for a local soup kitchen.

CALLING A HOUSE A HOME

One of the most ambitious things you can do to help the homeless is to build homes. This may sound far-fetched, but an organization called Habitat for Humanity does just that. This nonprofit organization has worked to help the homeless and impoverished since 1976. Since their founding, they have helped build or repair more than 600,000 homes. They have 1,500 local chapters and more than eighty international chapters around the world. Habitat for Humanity has helped millions of people around the world by building affordable housing from the ground up. Former President Jimmy Carter and his wife, Rosalynn Carter, actively support and participate in Habitat for Humanity by taking part in a different volunteer project with the organization each year.

While students may not be permitted to participate in all of the same tasks as adults, they can engage in light jobs, such as shoveling, hammering, measuring, and painting. In addition, Habitat for Humanity may be an excellent source for obtaining research, interviews, and information about the

There are several volunteer groups that are dedicated to helping the homeless by building houses or other structures.

needs of the community. There may be work that a service-learning group can do to promote a particular Habitat project or to raise community awareness of their projects.

HABITAT FOR HUMANITY

If you are interested in the work of Habitat for Humanity, you can look for a local affiliate near your community. Entering your zip code into their national website can help link you to a website made specifically for your community. The site will list projects that have been recently completed in your area. The site will likely indicate whether the affiliate office is accepting applications for building new structures. It may also show other projects that the Habitat affiliate is involved with, such as reduced furniture sales for families in need or scholarship programs for students from economically at-risk families.

RAISING AWARENESS, RAISING SPIRITS

Homelessness is one of the most difficult societal problems to solve. While students can contribute their time and resources to homeless shelters and soup kitchens, it is unlikely that they will be able to solve the root problems that are actually causing homelessness in the first place. However, students can do a lot to raise consciousness about the problem, educate the public, and become advocates for homelessness prevention.

Raising money for homeless shelters is certainly one idea that can benefit the homeless population. But more indirect approaches may be able to address the problem on a different level. Students can use their writing skills in a few areas to raise consciousness in their community. Submitting an editorial to your town's newspaper can provide residents with the benefit of your research about the history of homelessness. Writing a play that addresses the issue of homelessness can be a powerful form of communication as well. A service-learning project may involve organizing a play from beginning to end. Social studies research can be incorporated into the play's plot, character education can help with leadership, and organizational skills can assist in presenting the play to the public. Industrial arts students can contribute to stage scenery and props. And finally, math skills can be used to calculate ticket-sale profits that can be donated to a local homeless shelter.

While many of the ideas for helping the homeless involve indirect contact with the homeless, you can also deal directly with the homeless population in your area. Talk with someone in charge at a local homeless shelter to see if you can interview a homeless person. Perhaps the shelter director knows of someone who used to be homeless who can speak to your class about his or her experience. Work closely with a teacher to coordinate efforts involving the direct use of the homeless population, however. Your top priority is safety and to show personal respect.

Students directly involved in tackling the issue of homelessness may have some of the most rewarding experiences in service learning. Working with the homeless population can inspire students to consider pursuing a career in social work or community organizing. When students become involved in community service while they are still young, their horizons open, and they have the time to explore what might interest them when they are ready to think of a career.

Some schools are fortunate enough to include service learning as a part of their regular school curriculum. Other schools may be just beginning to explore service learning as an option. They may be in the early stages of exploring how to get students' attention and help them learn their school curriculum in an exciting new way. Or, perhaps you attend a school where service learning is not even a blip on the radar screen. Regardless of your school's situation, you can make an effort to bring service learning into your life.

Volunteerism is something that is traditionally not found in school curricula. You are more likely to see volunteerism as part of faith-based or scouting groups. However, students who do not join groups like these on their own time may be missing out on a life-altering experience. The rewards of helping those who are less fortunate can be far reaching and last a lifetime. Students can learn their "life's calling" when they volunteer and realize how it makes them feel about themselves and the world. Jack Hirsch, a former student of Piedmont Virginia Community College, was grateful for the opportunities he received through service-learning programs at the school. "There is no better way to learn about yourself, your community, and humanity in general than to get involved in some form of volunteerism," Hirsch states. "Much more, to me, it is a responsibility. It is a way to give back and show my gratitude for everything I have been given."

So, if you are in a school that does not already incorporate service learning, you may wish to take a few steps to get involved. With a few tips, getting started with service learning can be easier than you ever imagined.

LEADERSHIP QUALITIES

Introducing service learning to people around you means demonstrating to others that you are a good leader. Developing leadership skills is not an easy task, but these valuable traits can be applied throughout your life. Rosalynn Carter, former First Lady of the United States and an active volunteer in the organization Habitat for Humanity, stated, "A leader takes people where they want to go. A great leader takes people where they don't necessarily want to go, but ought to be." When you introduce service learning to others, you can make their lives richer. Service learning can help them realize what they can do to help their community. Your work can open their eyes to the problems that poor, hungry, and homeless people face every day. A leader brings people out of their comfort zone and guides them with loving care.

FIND A SCHOOL MENTOR

Finding a mentor may be the most important thing you do to get started with service learning. A mentor is an adult that you can look up to for advice and guidance. If you are interested in volunteering to help hungry and homeless people, consider what a social studies teacher can do in terms of mentoring. Social studies teachers may be familiar with the local and state

A teacher who serves as a mentor may know what is required to start a service-learning program in your school.

laws about vagrancy. Understanding the root causes of homelessness can help teachers incorporate programs into their curriculum. Teachers can look to their history standards to see how the topic fits in, or they can think about how they teach economics during the school year. Both hunger and homelessness have economic causes, and studying their histories can give teachers and students ideas about how to help their community.

Remember that you may find a mentor in the most unlikely places. Think about which teachers you admire most or have the best relationships with. Regardless of that teacher's subject, you may simply have a better rapport when planning a project. This can help shape how you approach your service-learning proposal to the school. For example, suppose you have a good relationship with your industrial arts teacher or your drama teacher. If that person is receptive to working on a service-learning plan for the school, tailor it around the subject that educator teaches. You may think about making storage units for a food pantry with the industrial arts class. You may wish to put together a consciousness-raising play with the drama class. Start with what's easy and attainable.

If you can't find a teacher who is as interested in service learning as you are, don't worry. You may be able to approach a guidance counselor to introduce the idea of a service-learning program at your school. Remember that classroom teachers have many responsibilities between preparing class lectures, grading homework, and other school obligations. They may not have time for the extra commitment. Always keep in mind the commitment that service learning requires. Teachers need to coordinate efforts, keep students safe, and also assess students on each level of the project. Even if a teacher is interested in doing these things, it is up to the school to decide whether the teacher is allowed to take part.

TAKE THE PROPER CHANNELS

Showing your interest and taking action on a small scale can help spread the word about service-learning projects. The beginning stages may be difficult, and the project may be hard to get off the ground, but remember that you will have something to show when you are finished, The demonstration stage of service learning can help teach others what you learned and pique the interest of other students. As you face obstacles in your organization stages, keep the end product in mind.

Once you have found a mentor or guidance counselor who is as excited about service learning as you are, it's time to take the proper channels and get a small-scale program approved. Your adult adviser should be able to talk to supervisors to let them know about your plans and what may be involved in the process. Be prepared and willing to write a proposal to a school principal or superintendent. Your willingness to show initiative can help school administrators decide to take a chance with something new. Taking the proper channels will show your leadership skills and prove that you

A teacher can help you write a proposal for a service-learning program if one does not already exist in your school.

are dedicated to volunteerism and helping hungry and homeless people.

FIND LIKE-MINDED SOULS

Even if you show great leadership skills and have terrific ideas about helping the community, there's no reason to go it alone. In fact, showing that you can work with others is necessary if you want to help the community and work with the public. Find some friends or other classmates who have similar interests as you. You may present your desire to get involved in service learning to a student government group. There, you may find other students who are dedicated to helping the community. Working together will help you reach your goal faster and more easily.

Remember that service learning requires teamwork in each of the five steps: investigation, planning, action, reflection, and demonstration. During the investigation stage, students brainstorm ideas and research them. Doing this alone would result in a narrower view of your possibilities. Other students may come up with ideas that you would have never dreamed of, and they may have personal experiences that can add to the group's investigations. During the planning stage, the need for many hands may become apparent. Service-learning projects can be daunting! You may require each student in class to handle many tasks in order to accomplish your goal. The planning stage is a time when you can work with others to decide whether your ideas are realistic and possible for your team. After your team works together to take action in the community, reflection can be helpful on a group level. Bouncing memories off of each other can help spur ideas about how your work helped the community. Reflecting about the state of hunger and homelessness in your community, state, nation, and the world is a discussion worth having on a large scale. Work with your group to understand the most you can about your project. Gaining insights from

Sharing ideas and plans among the other students in your group will benefit your service-learning project. Everyone has different insights that will improve the experience.

others can lead you to understand the issues in greater detail or from different angles.

LOOK OUTSIDE SCHOOL

Trying to get your school involved in a service-learning project for the first time can be a challenge, and there's no guarantee of success. If you think you've exhausted all of the avenues available to you at your school, look to other resources for help and guidance from adults. Boy Scout or Girl Scout troops are often extremely dedicated to community service and volunteering. If you do not already belong to a troop in your area, contact your local council and ask about how you can bring your idea to a local troop. You are likely to find a dedicated and experienced adult who knows how to coordinate volunteer projects with the local community.

Asking for donations from the community is a good way to get dedicated adults involved in helping to organize service-learning projects.

In order to earn the highest honor in scouting—the Eagle Award in Boy Scouts and the Gold Award in Girl Scouts—an extensive community service project is required. A service-learning project can be a good opportunity for scouts to explore the issues of hunger and homelessness in their communities and come up with a plan that can help those in need. The rewards can be much more than a patch or a medal. The project can get the whole troop involved and become a great way for a scout troop to bond, learn, and grow as a group. Incorporating different curriculum areas can be coordinated with troop leaders so that badges can be earned for other scouts in the areas of economics, gardening, volunteerism, or community service. Fundraising can be done as a troop, as necessary, and investigative research about social issues can be undertaken with the guidance of a troop leader.

> TAKE THE COLLEGE ROUTE

If you don't feel experienced enough to start a service-learning opportunity on your own, research service-learning departments at local colleges. Many colleges have service-learning departments with community projects planned throughout the year. These departments are designed for students who wish to pursue a career in service learning, and they may have opportunities for younger students to get involved and help during various stages of the process.

Another option is to work through a faith-based or other youth group. Many faith-based youth organizations do regular service with the poor, and this may include hungry and homeless people. Groups such as these are great places to start an investigation into hunger and homelessness issues and what the group has experienced through their volunteerism. Introduce the idea of service learning to a pastor or youth-group leader. Some of these leaders are experienced teachers who may already be familiar with the curricula that should be covered in school. They may have their own ideas about how different curriculum areas can be met through a service-learning project that aids the homeless population or food-insecure families in the area.

BE A RESOURCE HOUND

Even after you have found a group who can work through a service-learning project with you, keep looking for resources that can guide you through the process. A school district or scouting office may be a good place to start. For example, a Chicago, Illinois, public school district has organized many resources for people interested in service learning. Coalition for the Homeless, the U.S. Department of Housing and Urban Development, the Salvation Army, and the National Alliance to End Homelessness are all recommended as places where student can serve, research, or find experienced people to interview.

CHAPTER FIVE

A LIFETIME OF LEARNING

According to the National Alliance to End Homelessness, there are between 2.5 million and 3.5 million people who either live on the streets in the United States or require the use of emergency shelters. On any given night, about 750,000 people are homeless. A full 23 percent of these people are chronically homeless. According to the Department of Housing and Urban Development, a chronically homeless person is someone who has been without a home for a year or longer. A chronically homeless person can also be someone who has had at least four episodes of homelessness in the past three years. While any bout of homelessness is devastating, the chronically homeless are the most vulnerable in our society. Community service that seeks to help these vulnerable populations can mean an improved society and a better place to live for all residents.

The statistics on hunger also tell a difficult story. Having forty-nine million people living in food-insecure

The lines for admission to homeless shelters have grown increasingly longer. As poverty levels rise in the United States, the need for service-learning projects for the hungry and homeless is more important than ever.

households in one of the richest nations in the world is an unacceptable statistic. Having nearly sixteen million children without regular access to the foods they need to grow indicates that a serious problem exists. Service that seeks to help hungry people shows compassion and dedication to the community, as well as the nation as a whole.

Service learning can shine a light on difficult topics such as poverty, unemployment, urban housing issues, substance abuse, veteran issues, and mental health issues. A study of the hungry or homeless population in a community can point to these issues as contributing factors. Students who take part in service learning should keep their eyes and ears open to the common causes of the problems they are trying to solve. Ending hunger means understanding why people are going without food in the first place. Ending homelessness means understanding the root causes of homelessness. Service learning is a great place to begin a lifetime of learning about social issues.

> IT'S MORE THAN A GRADE

Some students look at service learning as just another grade they must earn in school. When they go through the experience, however, they are often transformed by what they see, do, and learn. Students realize that service learning is more than just another grade on their report card. It provides an experience they can reflect on and learn from. It's a way to get out of the classroom and into the real world.

KEEP IT SAFE

When going out into the public for service-learning experiences, there are a few things to keep in mind. First, you will no longer be on school property. You will likely need parental permission to take part in these programs and leave school grounds to volunteer at shelters or food pantries.

Second, safety is an important issue when working with the public. As with any time you go out in public, use common sense. For safety reasons, your school likely will not allow you to go to service facilities by yourself. Respect this decision, and understand that

Safety is key when working with the public. Working together with school groups can make the experience more enjoyable and safer than working alone.

your safety is of paramount importance. Work with a buddy, travel in groups, and understand that you need to have an adult present.

Citizens who use the services of food pantries or homeless shelters may have experienced difficult challenges in their lives. Their circumstances may be uncomfortable for some students who are working as volunteers. This is one reason the reflection stage should be stretched through the duration of the service-learning experience. Talking with other classmates about the people you meet can be important for some students' ability to process the experience. Teachers can also add valuable insight to the reflection stage, so listen to what they have to say about the community you are helping.

CAREERS IN COMMUNITY SERVICE

Suppose you take part in a service-learning experience and decide that you want to pursue community service more deeply. This has happened to many people who have given the experience a try. Maggie Castro worked on a service-learning project as part of Piedmont Virginia Community College. As a result, she decided what she wanted to do as a career. "I participate in service learning at an after school program at Sutherland Middle School every Tuesday and Thursday. Through working with these kids and teachers," she stated on the school's website, "I've realized that I want to have an instrumental part in the lives of teens. Service learning has broadened my horizons and truly taught me more about other people in my community."

There are many jobs and career paths for people who are interested in serving their community. Here are just a few ideas that can help you think about combining community service with a career path.

SERVICE-LEARNING SPECIALIST

Ten years ago, people would likely not have heard of a job specializing in service learning. But now, the educational approach to serving the community is

Professionals with the Department of Housing and Urban Development interview the homeless to understand their problems so they can try to address them.

experiencing a boom. More and more schools are incorporating the practice in their schools, and the need for experts in the field is expanding. Some departments of education, such as those in Maryland and Illinois, have blazed a trail for service-learning specialists. Cities such as Chicago have service-learning curriculums for their schools, and Maryland became the first state to require high school students to take part in service learning in order to graduate. The practice has also taken hold in Canadian schools and universities. The more this practice grows, the greater demand there will be for service-learning specialists.

SOCIAL WORKER

Social workers are people who are trained to help various suffering populations of people. They may have experience with community service and understand the problems associated with hungry, homeless, mentally ill, or drug-addicted populations. Many social workers work one-on-one with people who require emotional support or assistance with basic life skills. A social worker can make a difference in the lives of individuals who are experiencing the stresses of poverty, hunger, or homelessness.

FUNDRAISER

People who work on social programs know that a lack of funding can stand in the way of making a program truly valuable for the public. Some people specialize in fundraising and make a career out of raising money for social programs, charities, and nonprofit organizations.

COMMUNITY ORGANIZER

A community organizer is someone who helps community members work together to achieve common goals. President Barack Obama worked as a community organizer in Chicago, helping low-income neighborhoods meet their needs for housing, jobs, and many other issues. A community organizer may work with various organizations in the neighborhood, depending on the specific issues that need to be addressed. These could include unionization of local workers, improved garbage collection or sanitation practices, safety issues in schools, and neighborhood crime or homelessness reduction.

REFLECTING

Indian civil-rights leader Mahatma Gandhi once said, "The best way to find yourself is to lose yourself in the service of others." One way to test this idea is to get involved in service learning, whether you are taking part in the projects your school has developed or crafting your own ideas to explore. Seeing hungry and homeless people on the streets of your community can make some people feel like they want to spring to action. It can make others feel hopeless.

Don't feel hopeless about problems in society. Instead, do something to help, but realize that the

There are many ways that service learning can help the nation's hungry and homeless. At the same time, students acquire new skills and learn more about their community.

work won't be easy. As President Barack Obama once said about service, "The best way to not feel hopeless is to get up and do something. Don't wait for good things to happen to you. If you go out and make some good things happen, you will fill the world with hope, you will fill yourself with hope." Service learning is a great way to meet your school curriculum, learn, and fill the world with hope.

GLOSSARY

advocacy Public support for a particular cause or policy.

chronic homelessness The condition of being continuously homeless for a year or more, or having at least four episodes of homelessness in three years. To be considered chronically homeless, a person must have a disabling condition, such as a substance abuse problem, serious mental illness, or chronic physical illness.

community organizer A person who coordinates efforts of community members to improve the conditions of his or her neighborhood.

curriculum The subjects and content that make up a course of study at a school.

direct service Community service in which someone works directly with a community on a one-on-one basis, such as serving food or helping at a shelter.

Farm Bill A law that regulates farm prices, food production, and other food-related issues.

food desert An urban area or rural town without sufficient sources for buying affordable, high-quality, fresh food.

food insecurity Household condition in which occupants live in hunger or fear of starvation due to poverty or other conditions.

Habitat for Humanity An international nonprofit organization dedicated to building or repairing low-income housing to deal with homelessness and housing issues worldwide.

Hull House Settlement house in Chicago, Illinois, founded by Jane Addams and Ellen Gates Starr in

1889 to meet the housing needs of recently arrived European immigrants.

indirect service Community service in which someone helps the community, but not through working directly with community members.

legislation Laws written and passed by state or federal government.

mentor An experienced and trusted adviser to a less-experienced person.

nonprofit organization An organization that uses surplus revenues to meet goals rather than to profit.

service learning A method of teaching and learning that combines classroom instruction with meaningful community service.

social worker Someone employed to provide services to community members in need.

Supplemental Nutrition Assistance Program (SNAP) A government program, popularly known as food stamps, in which financial aid is provided for low- and no-income people for purchasing food.

sustainable Able to be maintained over a long period; not temporary.

vagrancy The state of living as a homeless, or vagrant, person.

vulnerable population Group of people suffering or at risk of suffering due to various conditions such as poverty, mental illness, or substance abuse.

FOR MORE INFORMATION

Action Against Hunger
247 West 37th Street, 10th Floor
New York, NY 10018
(212) 967-7800
Website: http://www.actionagainsthunger.org
Action Against Hunger is an international humanitarian
    organization that aids malnourished children and
    attempts to ensure safe water and sustainable
    solutions to hunger.

Empty Bowls
P.O. Box 1689
Burnsville, NC 28714
(828) 675-9636
Website: http://www.emptybowls.net
Empty Bowls is a nonprofit organization and
    grassroots effort to raise money and awareness
    of the issue of hunger by providing models for
    aiding the community.

Feeding America
35 East Wacker Drive, Suite 2000
Chicago, IL 60601
(800) 771-2303
Website: http://feedingamerica.org
Feeding America is a hunger-relief charity with a
    nationwide network of food banks that help com-
    munities and fight to end hunger.

Food Banks Canada
5025 Orbitor Drive

Building 2, Suite 400
Mississauga, ON L4W 4Y5
Canada
(905) 602-5234
Website: http://www.foodbankscanada.ca
Food Banks Canada is the country's national charitable organization that represents and supports food banks across Canada by running programs, building partnerships, and raising awareness of the problems of hunger in Canada.

Habitat for Humanity International
121 Habitat Street
Americus, GA 31709
(800) HABITAT
Website: http://www.habitat.org
Habitat for Humanity is an international nonprofit organization that builds and repairs houses around the world using volunteer labor and donations.

National Coalition for the Homeless
2201 P Street NW
Washington, DC 20037
(202) 462-4822
Website: http://nationalhomeless.org
The National Coalition for the Homeless is a network of people who are currently experiencing homelessness or who have been homeless in the past, along with community activists and advocates working to help end homelessness in America.

Raising the Roof
263 Eglinton Avenue West, Suite 200
Toronto, ON M4R 1B1
Canada
(416) 481-1838
Website: http://www.raisingtheroof.org
Raising the Roof is an organization dedicated to pro-
    viding long-term solutions to Canada's homeless
    problem through fundraising, community service,
    and public education.

Stand Up for Kids
83 Walton Street, Suite 300
Atlanta, GA 30303
(800) 365-4KID
Website: http://www.standupforkids.org
Stand Up for Kids is a nonprofit organization aimed
    at ending homelessness among youth and teens
    in the United States, including runaways and
    at-risk populations.

Stop Hunger Now
615 Hillsborough Street, Suite 200
Raleigh, NC 27603
(919) 839-0689
Website: http://www.stophungernow.org
Stop Hunger Now is an international relief organiza-
    tion that distributes food and aid to vulnerable
    populations around the world.

Volunteers of America
1660 Duke Street

Alexandria, VA 22314
(800) 899-0089
Website: http://www.voa.org
Volunteers of America is a nonprofit organization operating in over four hundred communities in forty-six states, the District of Columbia, and Puerto Rico to aid vulnerable populations, including hungry and homeless people.

WEBSITES

Because of the changing nature of Internet links, Rosen Publishing has developed an online list of websites related to the subject of this book. This site is updated regularly. Please use the following link to access the list:

http://www.rosenlinks.com/SLFT/Hung

FOR FURTHER READING

Beckman, David. *Exodus from Hunger: We Are Called to Change the Politics of Hunger.* Louisville, KY: Westminster John Knox Press, 2010.

Boles, Nicole Bouchard. *How to Be an Everyday Philanthropist: 330 Ways to Make a Difference in Your Home, Community, and World—at No Cost!* New York, NY: Workman Publishing Company, 2009.

Burt, Alan R. *Blessings of the Burden: Reflections and Lessons in Helping the Homeless.* Grand Rapids, MI: William B. Eerdmans Publishing Company, 2013.

Carter, Jimmy. *If I Had a Hammer: Stories of Building Homes and Hope with Habitat for Humanity.* Somerville, MA: Candlewick, 2010.

Cress, Christine M., and Peter J. Collier. *Learning Through Service: A Student Guidebook for Service-Learning and Civic Engagement Across Academic Disciplines and Cultural Communities.* Sterling, VA: Stylus Publishing, 2012.

Dolgon, Corey W., and Christopher W. Baker. *Social Problems: A Service Learning Approach.* Thousand Oaks, CA: Sage Publications, 2010.

Donovan, Sandy. *Volunteering Smarts: How to Find Opportunities, Create a Positive Experience, and More* (USA Today Teen Wise Guides: Lifestyle Choices). Springfield, MO: 21st Century, 2012.

Farber, Katy. *Change the World with Service Learning: How to Create, Lead, and Assess Service Learning Projects.* Lanham, MD: R&L Education, 2011.

Friedman, Jenny, and Jolene Roehlkepartain. *Doing Good Together: 101 Easy, Meaningful Service Projects for Families, Schools, and Communities.* Minneapolis, MN: Free Spirit Publishing, 2010.

Kendricks, Kevin D. *Open Our Eyes: Seeing the Invisible People of Homelessness* (In the News). Seattle, WA: CreateSpace Independent Publishing Platform, 2010.

Lewis, Barbara A. *The Teen Guide to Global Action: How to Connect with Others (Near & Far) to Create Social Change.* Minneapolis, MN: Free Spirit Publishing, 2007.

Loeb, Paul Rogat. *Soul of a Citizen: Living with Conviction in Challenging Times.* New York, NY: St. Martin's Griffin, 2010

Marcovitz, Hal. *Teens & Volunteerism.* Broomall, PA: Mason Crest, 2013.

Ryan, Kevin. *Almost Home: Helping Kids Move from Homelessness to Hope.* New York, NY: Wiley, 2012.

Sagawa, Shirley. *The American Way to Change: How National Service and Volunteers Are Transforming America.* New York, NY: Jossey-Bass, 2010.

Singer, Peter. *The Life You Can Save: Acting Now to End World Poverty.* New York, NY: Random House, 2009.

Strait, Jean R., and Marybeth Lima. *The Future of Service-Learning: New Solutions for Sustaining and Improving Practice.* Sterling, VA: Stylus Publishing, 2009.

Sundem, Garth. *Real Kids, Real Stories, Real Change: Courageous Actions Around the World.* Minneapolis, MN: Free Spirit Publishing, 2010.

Wilson, Michael R., M.D. *Hunger: Food Insecurity in America* (In the News). New York, NY: Rosen Publishing, 2009.

Winne, Mark. *Closing the Food Gap: Resetting the Table in the Land of Plenty.* Boston, MA: Beacon Press, 2009.

BIBLIOGRAPHY

Cadena, Christine. "Service-Learning in Local Homeless Shelters: Impacts on College Student Success." Yahoo! Voices, August 22, 2008. Retrieved February 8, 2014 (http://voices .yahoo.com/service-learning-local-homeless -shelters-1839258.html?cat=72).

Chicago Alliance to End Homelessness. "Homeless Stats." Retrieved February 10, 2014 (http://www. thechicagoalliance.org/homelessstats.aspx).

Chicago Public Schools. "Housing and Homeless- ness Resource Guide." Retrieved February 2, 2014 (http://www.servicelearning.cps.k12.il.us/ pdf/housingResource.pdf).

Corporation for National and Community Service. "Leg- islation." Retrieved February 8, 2014 (http://www .nationalservice.gov/about/legislation).

DoSomething.org. "11 Facts About Hunger in the U.S." Retrieved February 8, 2014 (http://www.dosome- thing.org/tipsandtools/11-facts-about-hunger-us).

Food Banks Canada. "About Hunger in Canada." Retrieved February 8, 2014 (http://www .foodbankscanada.ca/Learn-About-Hunger/ About-Hunger-in-Canada.aspx).

Goodreads. "Quotes About Service." Retrieved February 10, 2014 (http://www.goodreads.com/quotes/tag/ service).

Kaye, Cathryn Berger, and Maureen Connolly. "With Common Core State Standards, Why Service Learn- ing Matters Even More." National Association of Secondary School Principals, May 2013. Re- trieved February 3, 2014 (http://www.nassp.org/

tabid/3788/default.aspx?topic=With_Common_Core_State_Standards_Why_Service_Learning_Matters_Even_More).

Kids Consortium. "Examples of Service-Learning Projects." Retrieved February 10, 2014 (http://www.kidsconsortium.org/minigrantprojectexamples.php).

Kruse, Kevin. "100 Best Quotes on Leadership." Forbes.com, November 16, 2012. Retrieved February 10, 2014 (http://www.forbes.com/sites/kevinkruse/2012/10/16/quotes-on-leadership).

Maryland State Department of Education. "Poverty." Retrieved February 8, 2014 (http://www.marylandpublicschools.org/MSDE/programs/service-learning/poverty.html).

Maryland State Department of Education. "Service Learning in Maryland." Retrieved February 8, 2014 (http://www.marylandpublicschools.org/msde/programs/servicelearning).

Missouri State University. "Student Testimonials." Citizenship and Service-Learning. Retrieved February 8, 2014 (http://www.missouristate.edu/casl/54229.htm).

National Youth Leadership Council. "Programs." Retrieved February 3, 2014 (http://www.nylc.org/programs).

Piedmont Virginia Community College. "Service Learning Testimonials." Retrieved February 9, 2014 (http://www.pvcc.edu/service_learning/testimonials.php).

San Diego Unified School District. "Learn and Serve San Diego." Retrieved February 8, 2014 (http://www.sandi.net/cms/lib/CA01001235/

Centricity/Domain/62/Current%20CRD%20
Web%20Docs/Elementary%20Handbook%20Re-
vised%20July%2010.pdf).

Saunders, Stephen. "Jane Addams Hull House Is
Closing Its Doors." ChicagoBusiness.com, January
19, 2012. Retrieved February 9, 2014 (http://
www.chicagobusiness.com/article/20120119/
BLOGS03/120119750/jane-addams-hull-house-is-
closing-its-doors#)

Sloan, Willona M. "Integrating Service Learning into
the Curriculum." Association for Supervision and
Curriculum Development, January 2008. Retrieved
February 4, 2014 (http://www.ascd.org/publications/
newsletters/education-update/jan08/vol50/num01/
Integrating-Service-Learning-into-the-Curriculum.aspx).

Statistic Brain. "Homelessness/Poverty Stats."
Retrieved February 8, 2014 (http://www.statistic
brain.com/homelessness-stats)

Study in the USA. "Learn, Lead, Serve: Service-Learning
in the United States." Retrieved February 8, 2014
(http://studyusa.com/en/a/50/learn-lead-serve:-
service-learning-in-the-united-states).

INDEX

ABOUT THE AUTHOR

Kathy Furgang is a writer who has written educational books for teens for many years. She has written about volunteerism and internship programs in various professions. She also writes for teacher guides and textbooks for students in elementary and middle school.

PHOTO CREDITS

Cover Monkey Business Images/Shutterstock.com; p. 3 bymandesigns/Shutterstock.com; pp. 4–5 Anton Oparin/Shutterstock.com; p. 8 FuzzBones/Shutterstock.com; pp. 9, 12, 18, 31 © AP Images; p. 16 Commercial Eye/The Image Bank/Getty Images; p. 22 © iStockphoto.com/eurobanks; p. 23 Charles Sykes/Invision/AP Images; pp. 26, 61 The Washington Post/Getty Images; p. 29 Curve/Vetta/Getty Images; p. 33 Flashon Studio/Shutterstock.com; p. 34 Milos Bicanski/Getty Images; p. 35 © William Camargo/ZUMA Press; pp. 39, 53 Steve Debenport/E+/Getty Images; pp. 41, 50 Hero Images/Getty Images; p. 45 Antonio Guillem/Shutterstock.com; pp. 47, 59 Ariel Skelley/Blend Images/Getty Images; p. 52 Blend Images/Hill Street Studios/Brand X Pictures/Getty Images; p. 56 Tom Wang/Shutterstock.com; p. 57 Justin Sullivan/Getty Images; p. 64 © The U-T San Diego/ZUMA Press; cover and interior pages background textures and patterns vector illustration/Shutterstock.com, Apostrophe/Shutterstock.com, nattanan726/Shutterstock.com, Yulia Glam/Shutterstock.com; back cover silhouette Pavel L Photo and Video/Shutterstock.com.

Designer: Michael Moy; Editor: Christine Poolos; Photo Researcher: Karen Huang